EDUCATING FOR ETERNITY

Educating for Eternity

CLAUDE E. SCHINDLER, JR.
&
PACHECO PYLE

TYNDALE HOUSE
PUBLISHERS, INC.
WHEATON, ILLINOIS

SCRIPTURE QUOTATIONS IN THIS BOOK
ARE FROM THE KING JAMES VERSION
EXCEPT WHERE OTHERWISE INDICATED.

LIBRARY OF CONGRESS CATALOG CARD NUMBER 78-68907
ISBN 0-8423-0678-1
COPYRIGHT © BY CLAUDE E. SCHINDLER, JR. AND PACHECO PYLE
FIRST PRINTING, AUGUST 1979
PRINTED IN THE UNITED STATES OF AMERICA
OCTOBER 1979

CONTENTS

1
Purpose

THE JUVENILE DETENTION CENTER: A drab place for distressed youngsters. In a counseling room I sat across from a young man who was gifted with a well-developed intellect. He had been reared by loving Christian parents. He himself claimed to know Jesus Christ personally; yet he was a runaway. His *spirit,* the part of a believer where the Holy Spirit resides,[1] was not in control of his attitudes and actions; instead, his *natural mind* was in charge.

I thought about what Christian thinker Watchman Nee once wrote: "The spirit and the soul are two totally different organs; one belongs to God while the other belongs to man."[2] The mind resides in the soul of man and, in the case of this young man, was in complete control. He had a secular, humanistic outlook. His mind was educated from a godless and man-centered view of life.

I left that place more determined than ever to use every means I could find to convince parents, pastors, teachers, and administrators that we must develop young people who are Christ-centered, young people who are strong in spirit and whose spirits are in charge of their minds.

An ambitious goal! How can it be reached in our materialistic, sense-oriented, pleasure-mad society?

To begin with, by the decision of this nation's Supreme Court our public schools are forbidden to deal with the spiritual needs of our children. They are committed to developing the intellect without guidance from or reference to the Holy Spirit, who, the Scripture says, "will guide you into all truth."[3] Public schools are encouraged to guide students in developing academically, physically, and even socially. But what of the part of the child that lives forever? There is no provision for speaking to the student's spiritual needs. Since 1963, Christian teachers and administrators in public schools have been restricted from helping a child to satisfy the longings of his spirit, that part of him that communicates with his Maker. His view of the world and of life is thus man-centered, not God-centered.

Christian parents across the nation, recognizing that the best waking hours of a child are spent in the classroom, have begun searching out Christian schools. Where there is none, many parents are working to start one. This trend has grown so prevalent that on the average two new Christian schools are started somewhere in our nation every day.[4]

Yet even our Christian schools can be guilty of concentrating on helping the student "adjust" to this world, instead of helping him develop the *wisdom* and *understanding* that lead a student to become pure in character and strong in spirit.

Wisdom. Understanding. Those were the two qualities that Solomon requested of the Lord.[5] And God commended him for his sense of priority.

Wisdom. Understanding. These two qualities are extolled as being better than silver and gold, more precious than rubies, a tree of life, grace, safety.[6]

The book of Proverbs tells us, "Wisdom is the principal thing; therefore get wisdom: and with all thy getting get understanding."[7]

What is wisdom? It can be defined as looking

at life through God's eyes, solving problems as God solves them, having the mind of God, the mind of Christ.[8]

Understanding may be defined as the *application* of wisdom to our individual situations.

From my experience as superintendent of Dayton Christian Schools, a free-standing, inter-denominational corporation that ministers to some 1,495 students in kindergarten through grade 12, and from the observations I have made in other Christian schools (as President of the Ohio Association of Christian Schools), I want to suggest some scriptural approaches that will help young people become strong in spirit.

But first, let me briefly trace the history of education in this country so that we can understand why Christian families face a definite need for an alternative to public education.

2
How We Got Where We Are

THE ORIGINAL SCHOOLS IN THIS COUNTRY date back to the early seventeenth century. The motive for founding these schools was religious. Parents wanted their children to learn to read so that they could read the Bible.

The early history of our country and the attitudes of our early Presidents showed a great respect for the Word of God. Andrew Jackson said, "It is the rock upon which our republic rests." Herbert Hoover said, "There is no other book so various as the Bible, nor one so full of concentrated wisdom." George Washington said, "Above all, the pure and deifying light of revelation has had an influence on mankind and increased the blessings of society." Zachary Taylor said, "It was for the love of the truths of the great and good Book that our fathers abandoned their native shore for this wilderness." Abraham Lincoln said, "The first and almost the only book deserving of universal attention is the Bible. I speak as a man of the world and I say to you, 'Search the Scriptures.' " Woodrow Wilson said, "When you have read the Bible, you will know that it is the Word of God because you have found in it the key to your own heart and your own happiness and your own duty." Even Thomas Jefferson, hardly a fundamentalist, once stated, "I always have said and always will say, that the studious perusal of the sacred volume will make better citizens, better fathers, and better husbands."

It was not until the mid-nineteenth century that a push began for state-supported schools. This drive was led by Horace Mann, who believed that more children should have an opportunity for education. In appealing for the establishment of tax-supported schools, he said, "If the American taxpayers could collectively provide education for every child in America, within a short period of time the effect of the public school system would empty all the jails and prisons in the country." He told the legislators that in the long run a public school system would save the taxpayers money because the need for jails and prisons would be drastically reduced. Mann also suggested, "Let the home and the church teach faith and values, and the school will teach facts."[1]

The results of the tax-supported school and the consequent issue of separation of church and state were not immediately apparent, because until the turn of the century the great majority of American schoolteachers were committed to Protestant theism. (It is interesting to note that one of the historical reasons for the origin of the Roman Catholic school system was the Catholic conviction that the tax-supported schools were, in fact, Protestant.[2]) The personal conviction of these Christian teachers delayed the progress of secularization. Then in 1958 Dr. Jacob Getzels of the University of Chicago wrote of a new breed of teacher. Said Dr. Getzels, "Taking the place of puritan morality or moral commitment as a value, these new teachers hold relativistic moral attitudes without strong personal commitments. Absolutes in right or wrong are questionable. In a sense, morality has become a statistical rather than an ethical concept. Morality is what the group thinks is moral."[3]

Yet statistical morality is unthinkable for the

Christian because the absolutes of God's Word do not change.[4] I faced a classic example of this type of "changing ethics" or "situational ethics" in a class at a state university while studying for my Master's degree in education. The group was given the case of a mother during wartime who had no way to secure food for her children. Then the proposition was put forth that in such a case, wouldn't it be "moral" for her to sell her body in order to be able to feed her children? The class, made up of teachers and administrators from area public schools, agreed that in that case sexual immorality would be expedient. In the entire class, only one Catholic nun and I disagreed with the solution because it violated biblical principles.

When this new type of teacher came on the scene, the Supreme Court on June 17, 1963, ruling on the Abington Township Case, made the decision concerning prayer and Bible reading in the classroom. In effect, the ruling was that because of the pluralism of our society, and because of the desire for separation of church and state, the classroom must remain neutral.

But religious neutrality in the public schools is impossible. We can separate church and state, but we cannot separate religion and education. The ultimate end of education, the nature of persons educated, the nature of truth: all these are religious questions requiring religious answers. The answers may issue from the religion of secularism, humanism, or pragmatism, or they may issue from the religion of Christianity; but they will be religious answers.

To illustrate the impossibility of separating

religion and education, I will refer to one more example that surfaced in a class I took while acquiring my Master's degree. In an advanced educational psychology course the professor asked the class what they thought the nature of man to be. Without exception that class of teachers and administrators defined the nature of man as good. When I tried to voice an exception by stating what the Bible says about man's nature, I was politely told that religious views were not to be brought up in the class. Yet those educators were completely contradicting God's assessment that man's heart is "desperately wicked."[5]

The Supreme Court further ruled on June 28, 1971, that all education is to be divided into secular and sacred. But the notion that "secular" education is devoid of religious values is a myth. John Blanchard asserts, "Secular education has its faith and its values, and these have a decided religious impact. The Supreme Court itself has said that the faith that there is no Supreme Being constitutes a religious conviction, and is to be respected as such. Secular education affirms in faith that 'in the beginning was chance,' that man is an animal, that truth is relative, and that death is the end. These are all articles of faith. Teaching of these articles of faith constitutes an establishment of religion. The use of tax money to support this significantly assails the constitutional rights of Bible-believing citizens. The constitutional rights of a significant number of citizens are being significantly assailed."[6]

Sadly, Horace Mann's dream of empty jails and prisons has turned into the nightmare of violence in the public schools themselves.

U.S. News & World Report (January 26, 1976) ran a special report on "Terror in Schools," saying, "What's happening in schools is more than a crime problem. . . . Violence and vandalism in the nation's public schools are approaching epidemic proportions—and nobody seems to know what to do about it.

"Investigating the scope of school crime, a Senate subcommittee found that, between 1970 and 1973:

School-related homicides increased by 18 percent.

Rapes and attempted rapes increased by 40 percent. Robberies went up 37 percent.

Assaults on students soared—up 85 percent.

Assaults on teachers also made a big jump—77 percent.

Drug and alcohol offenses on school property increased by 38 percent."[7]

In the Gallup Poll of the Public's Attitude toward the Public Schools (issued in October 1976), George Gallup commented: "Juvenile delinquency, increasing yearly, has focused attention upon the need for *moral education not only in the home but in the schools*" (emphasis mine).[8]

"Let the home and the church teach faith and values, and the school will teach facts," Mr. Mann had said. *It won't work.* You cannot remove the only source of absolutes and expect it to work. Permissiveness will follow.

In that same poll, the problems in public schools were ranked:

1. Lack of discipline
2. Integration/segregation/busing

19

3. Lack of proper financial support
4. Poor curriculum
5. Use of drugs
6. Difficulty of getting "good" teachers
7. Parents' lack of interest
8. Size of school/classes
9. School board policies
10. Pupils' lack of interest.[9]

Many parents today have memories of their own school days when they were instructed by wholesome teachers who at least respected the Christian faith, and many of whom were themselves born-again Christians. While there are some Christians still teaching in public schools, the only "slant" or philosophy that can be heartily endorsed by our present public school system is that which makes Man central in life and ignores or denies the existence of a Divine Creator.

John D. Jess puts it succinctly: "For nearly half a century students in our public schools have been nurtured on a behavioristic philosophy based on the following principles:

1. Man is supreme (therefore there is no Higher Power).
2. Man evolved from lower forms of life (therefore there was no act of creation).
3. Man is an animal (therefore he could not have a soul).
4. Man is inherently good (therefore he is not in need of a Savior).
5. Common practice sets the standard (therefore there are no moral absolutes).

6. Criminals are merely antisocial (therefore they are not sinners).
7. 'Maladjustment' explains all malevolent human behavior (therefore there is no such thing as guilt).
8. Bad environment is to blame for all evil (therefore man is not responsible)."[10]

Mr. Jess has well encapsulated the contents of the *Humanist Manifesto I and II,* signed by such influential educators as John Dewey and B.F. Skinner.

As Christian parents begin to recognize the ungodly pressures on their children's minds, they become increasingly concerned with an alternate form of education. Again quoting William J. Lanouette in *The National Observer,* the reasons parents give for putting their children in Christian schools include these:

"A desire to teach their children the 'three Rs' and other traditional academic skills.

A belief that the Bible and Christian traditions should be an integral part of all education.

A yearning for strict discipline, neat grooming and dress, and other firm reactions to public-school 'permissiveness.'

A fear of racial and social unrest.

A frustration with the recent directions and performance of public education.

An assumption that by withdrawing their children from public schools—which often are showcases for social change—their educations and formative experiences will be patterned along the traditional religious and social lines of the past."[11]

I want to make a comment about the "fear of racial and social unrest." Though in some sections of the country, private schools have been formed for the specific purpose of excluding blacks or other minorities, that is not the kind of Christian school I will be referring to in this book. At our own Dayton Christian Schools some fifteen percent of the student body is from minority races, most of them from among the black community.

Of course, as evangelical Christians, we are concerned with the needs of all of America's children; then the question naturally arises, "Is it fair for Christian parents to pull their children from the public school systems? Won't that remove the Christian witness from a place where it is desperately needed?"

I would like to approach that question from two angles: First, if the Christian schools are doing their job right, *more* will be added to the Church. I base that assertion on the experience of the early believers as recorded in the book of Acts. As they enjoyed fellowship with each other every day, studying together, praying together, their praises lifted up the Name of God; and the Lord added people to the Church *daily*.[12] Their very ability to be together daily, building one another up, resulted in a joyous faith that *attracted* outsiders to the Lord.

Also, that question was answered for me by Dr. Tim LaHaye, pastor, author, and Christian college president, when I interviewed him for a radio program in 1974:

"I'm so glad you asked me that question!" Dr. LaHaye said. "That's one of my pet peeves because it is 180 degrees in opposition to what I think is good, sound judgment.

"I have asked pastors, good men of God, 'Why do you make a different policy for children than you do for adults?' For example: If we want to send a missionary out to work among the uneducated Hottentots who cannot read or write, what do we do? We send him to a Christian college, to a seminary, on deputation, and after about nine years of preparation, we send him out to be a missionary.

"But when it comes to our 16-year-old children, we send them into public schools, untrained, unprepared, unequipped, and expect them to be missionaries. That is ridiculous! Jesus spent three years training men to be missionaries. How can we expect a kid of 15 or 16 to be a match for some mind-bender, some biology professor who has been 'over the road' and knows all the questions and the answers to make fools of our kids, and then surround them with drugs, dope, sex, etc. I think that is unwise and very shallow thinking."

Obviously, the best way for Christians to make an impact on the unbelieving world is for them to be totally convinced of their faith and totally committed to their Lord. The Scriptures do teach that it is a quality of children to be "tossed to and fro, and carried about with every wind of doctrine, by the sleight of men, and cunning craftiness, whereby they lie in wait to deceive."[13] Children are different from adults. They do not think and understand like adults. In 1 Corinthians 13:11 the Apostle Paul says, "When I was a child, I spake as a child, I understood as a child, I thought as a child: but when I became a man, I put away childish things." To say that children should be witnesses for Christ in our public schools is being naive. God created them in such a way as to want to please adults. It was God's plan from the very beginning that adults, mainly mothers and fathers, will be instrumental in forming their values, morals, and standards for life. Thus children, with great faith in their teachers, go to school to receive instruction, not to give forth.

Evangelical Christians are also concerned about the sheltering or "hothouse argument" for youngsters attending Christian schools. Will they be prepared to live in the world if they are not exposed to the "real world"? Well-known Christians have addressed themselves to this issue. Let me quote a few for you.

Dr. Theodore Epp: "The first time I heard that, it was from the Devil when he talked to Eve and said, 'You know, when you eat of the tree, you are going to know the difference between good and evil. You will no longer be sheltered the way you are now.' God wanted man to know only good, so Satan made it his purpose to see that man tasted evil. Satan's desire was to convince Eve that she lacked something because she knew only good. This kind of thinking is still with us today. An example of this is those who say they do not want to send their children to a Christian elementary school because they do not want to make house plants out of them. I believe such reasoning is completely out of line for the Christian because that kind of logic originated in Genesis 3 with Satan. Satan said to man in the Garden of Eden, 'God has made you a house plant. All you know is good. But you come with me and I will show you how you can be like God and know good and evil.' When presented to man in this way, evil's appeal was stronger than that of good. Man fell into sin and disobeyed God."[14]

Mr. Paul Harvey: "Years ago it was argued that students maturing in a sheltered environment would be like hothouse plants, be unprepared for the cold outside world. Now, more and more Americans are realizing that it is in fact the public or state school student who is over-protected. He is 'sheltered' from religious instruction and exposed to all forms of non-Christian philosophy and behavior."[15]

Dr. Roy Zuck: "It's a strange thing. Many Christian parents, who insist that their children go to Sunday school regularly and who try to teach them spiritual truths and values at home, are not sure that they should send their children to a Christian elementary school. For some reason, those parents seem to hesitate.

"I know. I used to think that way myself.

"I reasoned that Christians should seek to influence the public school system and not withdraw to cloistered schools. After all, I thought, how could a child learn to live for God in a secular world if he is confined only to a Christian environment? When would he learn to adjust to today's world? Wouldn't it be harmful for him to be sheltered in a 'hothouse' environment? Wouldn't an 'overdose' of Christian teaching possibly lead to an open rebellion against Christianity in his adolescent years?

"Then I realized a serious mistake in my logic. A hothouse is beneficial, not harmful, to young tender plants! They need protection, care, and nurture in their early days. This helps them become strong and sturdy. Likewise, children need the protection, care, and nurture of a Christian environment. . . . Children attending the secularized public school system are not being adjusted to the world. Instead they are being conformed to the world."[16]

One of the compromises that Pharaoh offered to Moses was the same one being offered Christian parents today. Pharaoh offered to let the adults go and worship God, but leave their children in Egypt (state schools), and Moses refused (Exodus 10:8–11). Satan knew then and he knows now that if he can control the minds of children for one generation, he has won a great victory. Satan knows that it would be one generation before God's witness is seriously limited on the earth.

One last word: Does our nation send its troops to be trained in combat by its enemies? Of course not! We train them ourselves and prepare them to be as strong as possible to face the foe.

How can we send our children to be trained by a system that is openly against what Christianity stands for, and expect them somehow to become strong Christian soldiers?

3
What Makes a School Christian?

WHAT MAKES A SCHOOL DISTINCTIVELY Christian? Is it a program that includes chapel and Bible courses? Is it having prayer in the class room?

As important as programs are, they are not the determining factors. In fact, Jesus, the Master Teacher, did most of his teaching along beaches or on hillsides or on dusty paths, using everyday life as a textbook.

A Christian school is far more than an educational program with a religious coating. A school that is truly Christian is first of all centered in the authority of the Scriptures and the Person of Jesus Christ. Every subject is shot through with the wonder of God's power and love.

How is this done? Aren't facts *facts*, whether a student is a believer or an atheist? Yes, but the interpretation of facts makes the difference between a life that is being prepared only for time and one that is being prepared for eternity. As Dr. Roy Zuck put it: "In science, Christian teachers refer to the Creator of the creation. In literature, Christian teachers evaluate man's writings by biblical standards. In music and art, Christian teachers uphold a wholesome expression consistent with Scripture. In health and hygiene, Christian teachers point out that man is God's creation 'fearfully and wonderfully made.' In social studies, Christian teachers help students understand God's view of the world's cultures, governments, and problems."[1]

The Christian school seeks to train its students to view the whole of life from God's perspective, not just from man's point of view. We have a solemn warning to "beware lest any man spoil you through philosophy and vain deceit, after the tradition of men, after the rudiments of the world, and not after Christ."[2] All philosophies narrow down to be either man-centered (humanist) or God-centered. The philosophy of the Christian school, and in fact the goal of every Christian, is to be conformed to the image (likeness) of Jesus, to think like him and to act like him (Romans 8:29). The Christian school in accomplishing this goal helps young people look at their world and evaluate it through the eyes of Jesus using scriptural standards. The school must help its students to develop a "biblical filter system." (See illustration.)

But to train students to be spiritually sensitive requires teachers who themselves are spiritually attuned. As Jay Adams put it: "The Christian school is no better than and, indeed, not different from, its teachers, because at bottom the school *is* its teachers."[3]

Dr. Frank Gaebelein states: "The fact is inescapable: the world view of the teacher, insofar as he is effective, gradually conditions the world view of the pupil. No man teaches out of a philosophical vacuum. In one way or another, every teacher expresses the convictions he lives by, whether they be spiritually positive or negative."[4]

"A pupil . . . after he has been fully trained, will be like his teacher."[5] This principle is true not just in academic knowledge, but in life-style. It's how the teacher responds to his own life situations that will be transmitted to the students. It's how the teacher handles his problems, his

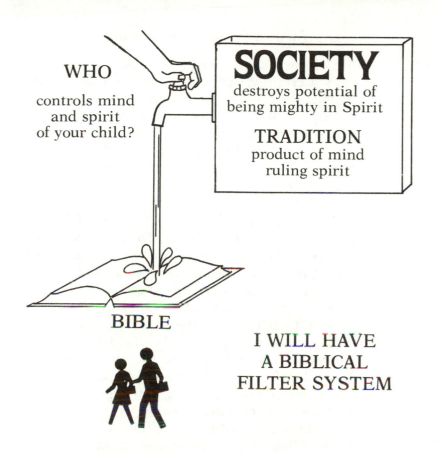

WHO

controls mind
and spirit
of your child?

SOCIETY

destroys potential of
being mighty in Spirit

TRADITION
product of mind
ruling spirit

BIBLE

I WILL HAVE
A BIBLICAL
FILTER SYSTEM

heartaches, his sins, his mistakes, and those people that despitefully use him—*that* is what is learned by the students. The students will become like the teacher in all ways.

Dr. Ron Chadwick, in a recent article published by the Western Association of Christian Schools (now part of the Association of Christian Schools International—ACSI), said this: "It has been estimated that the curriculum, in terms of courses, is only 10 percent of the impact in the life of the student, while the teacher is 90 percent. Certainly, what our children and young people need today is an adequate model—or example—of the reality of Jesus Christ."

A teacher has the very best hours of a child's life—when the child is awake, alert, and receptive. Jesus is the best example of the power of a teacher in the life of a student. A story in the fourth chapter of Acts vividly indicates that the fact of the disciples having *been with Jesus* changed their lives. As the enemies of the church observed the confidence of Peter and John and understood that they were uneducated (that is, formally untrained) men, they marveled and they recognized them as having *been with Jesus*. (It is interesting that the writer of the book of Acts pointed out specifically that they were uneducated, but that because they had been with Jesus they had great boldness and accomplished great things. They were truly strong in spirit and had wisdom and understanding!)

To illustrate further the influence of a teacher, I quote from the letter of one of our graduates who wrote from his Christian college:

> I'm preparing an article to be printed in our school paper about educating the "total man" . . . I feel so needed! Yet none of my suggestions are my own. It was those precious English classes with Mrs. E., science with Mr. M.; Mr. A., Mrs. P., Mrs. R., Mr. D., Mr. P., Mr. R., on and on and on—I think I feel like crying! The memories I have are not of pronouns, speech points, general science, Bible verses;

but of those times when someone cared to take an interest in my life. Even dear Miss M., as much as I hated her class I loved her! Now— with all those personalities and memories I am asked to give a little of what I've received. Almost commissioned by the Lord to bring it all here to help someone else grow. . . .

The whole teacher teaches the whole student. As a parent, I have observed the tremendous influence teachers have had on my children in establishing values and priorities in their lives.

When my eldest daughter entered the sixth grade, she had her first male teacher. She just about worshiped that man. Whatever he said was truth with a capital T. Since I have a background in mathematics, I used to sit down to help her with her math lessons. I didn't always use the same steps that she was learning in school. Though I would come up with the right answers, my daughter would look at me with her big blue eyes and say, "But, Daddy, Mr. R. says *this* is the way you do it!"

It made no difference what I said. That teacher had such an impact on her life that she was sure his way was the *only* way. My wife and I often said how grateful we were that Mr. R. was a man of God. What if he had been an unbeliever? Can you imagine how confusing such a situation would have been to my little girl?

A Christian school recognizes that the responsibility for training a child for its life requirements rests on the parents. And the parents have delegated the responsibility of formal education to the school. The school works *with* the home in building a foundation of spiritual and moral values, as well as in teaching basic skills.

A Christian school is *not* a substitute for the home or for the church. In fact, the child who benefits most from attending a Christian school is one who has parents who consistently teach and practice the way of the Lord at home, and who see to it that their family is actively involved in a Bible-teaching church. In no way can the school carry out spiritual training effectively without wholehearted support from the homes.

It is to the parents that God gave the directive in Deuteronomy 6:5-7, as paraphrased by Jay Adams: "Wherever you are, whatever you are doing, in all of life (when you are standing up, sitting down, walking, lying, in your house, wherever you are), in every life situation teach the Word of God by your words and examples, as it grows out of and applies to each situation."[6]

This is total life education. This is how God's commandments may be taught most effectively in the home and at school. The Christian school is God's vehicle for helping parents fulfill this directive.

There is more to say about what makes a school Christian, but that will come later.

4
How Do We Begin?

WHEN THERE IS NO CHRISTIAN SCHOOL IN an area, what can parents do?

Today there are Christian school associations that offer help. Some of them are:

American Association of Christian Schools
Association of Christian Schools International
Eastern Association of Christian Schools
National Association of Christian Schools
National Union of Christian Schools[1]

But in order to encourage those who are just beginning, I want to refer to the early years of Dayton Christian Schools (DCS), where I have served as superintendent since 1971.

The DCS story began on a Sunday night in the spring of 1963. The pastor of Patterson Park Grace Brethren Church, the church I attended, asked for those who might be interested in starting a Christian school to meet after the church service.

Christian school? Most of us didn't know anything about a Christian school—except for Sunday school, of course. Yet about fifteen people met that day, and a committee was appointed to study the feasibility of beginning a school to be sponsored by the church.

At that time I was manager of accounting and computer sales at the home offices of the National Cash Register Company. Educationally, I was a secular product, having graduated from Oakwood High School in Dayton and from the University of Cincinnati. I hadn't the foggiest notion of what a Christian school was; yet I was made chairman of the study committee. We proceeded to try to map strategy for a school beginning in September of that year with grades kindergarten through six.

Our committee brought in special speakers from other Christian day schools in Ohio. We investigated what would be required in the way of books, furniture, materials, and teachers—and got totally bogged down by the magnitude of the job.

There was just no way we could undertake such a task. I can remember calling the committee together for the last meeting with the definite intention of saying, "It is obviously not God's will for us to start a Christian school now because we can't get it off the ground. There's just too much involved."

Only two others showed up for the meeting, but one of them casually remarked, "In Vandalia, where I live, there are no public kindergartens. The schools have only grades 1 through 12. But some of the churches in the area have opened their facilities for kindergarten. Maybe we could begin like that?"

It was as though God had "switched on the light." Instantly, the three of us sensed that this idea was exactly the one we were to pursue.

The following fall, classes began in the basement of the church. Seventeen students and one teacher met on the first day of school to mark the beginning of Dayton Christian Schools, which now holds classes in several locations as a freestanding, interdenominational work. Our student body (pre-kindergarten through twelfth grade) now numbers almost 1,500, and we have a professional staff of seventy-six for the school year 1978–79.

The path from that time has seldom been smooth. In fact, the story of DCS is that of one impasse after another. Time after time we would reach the point of utter helplessness and hopelessness. And it seems to me that when we reached this point of frustration, God acted. It was as if he were reminding us that though human effort is important, no man can take the credit for accomplishing God's purposes.

For instance, by 1967 the school had outgrown the basement of the church. Yet expanding the church building was not practical because of the lack of land.

I was still with NCR at that time, but was also chairman of the school board. As we combed the area for other locations, we came up with one disappointment after another. The first involved acreage south of town which a man indicated he would *give* to the school. When word of his offer came out in the local newspaper, enthusiasm was high among the school families. Donated land! Now all we would have to do was build. But weeks passed, and no transaction took place. Finally we had to realize that the donor had changed his mind.

Then we heard of other acreage available at a good price. We quickly went out to look it over, our hopes high again. But it was so far from town that transportation would have presented great difficulties.

Humanly speaking, we tried everything in order to relocate; but it began to look as though there was no place for the school to go. Growth would have to stop.

At that point, God let us hear about the building he had for us. Through a sympathetic realtor we learned that a Seventh-Day Adventist school south of town with nine acres of land would be for sale. The property was not yet officially in any realtor's hands, so DCS was able to deal directly with the Adventists, thereby saving considerably on the price. The building and acreage were far better than *anything* we had seen before! And the location was less than two miles from the church where the school was then in session.

After signing an agreement to buy the campus for $324,000, we began trying to work out the financing. I recall that every place we looked, they said, "You can't do it." A bonding company, after looking at the school's records, said the consummation of the purchase was "not feasible." The school board members looked into selling bonds themselves, but that just never got off the ground.

Then we contacted the local bank where the school had its account. Two other board members and I had worked with the figures, carefully "massaging" them to reflect the school's and church's ability to handle the purchase, but the figures still showed a lack of $28,000 for the first year's payments. In the meeting with the bank officials, we were told, "We realize that you men talk about faith, but we're businessmen, and we work from a business standpoint, and from what we see, you can't handle this purchase. We have to base our decisions on that kind of thing, even though we'd like to help."

Following that statement, there was silence. Then one of us proposed: "If we can show you by next Tuesday that we can come up with $28,000 in pledges or some other way, will you give us the loan?"

The bankers agreed. After all, it was already Thursday, and how could this little school come up with such a large amount by the following Tuesday?

When the day arrived, we deposited $8,000 cash, with faith promises of $30,000. And to this day I'll never forget the expressions on the faces of those bankers—because I know they never thought we could do it. (They didn't know our *God*.) Now they had committed themselves, and it was the best possible loan: 7 percent, when all the bonding companies were talking eight and nine percent plus fees.

Even now, ten years later, the miracle of purchasing this campus on Wilmington Pike encourages us when our present path seems blocked.

Another circumstance in which God intervened involved the purchase of an adjoining nine acres in 1970. The Seventh-Day Adventists had tried to buy the surrounding property, but failed. In fact, the only reason they sold the Wilmington Pike campus was that the owners of the adjoining acreage had refused to sell, and the Adventists needed to expand.

The first summer that DCS occupied the campus, the church held a vacation Bible school there in the evenings. The owner of the adjoining property was a Christian, and he and his wife became so excited about the building being used at night as a Bible school that he offered to sell DCS nine acres with a two-story home for only $52,000. The church at that time was in no position to pay even this exceptional price. Because of this, four other Christian businessmen and I formed a corporation to buy the property for the school. Now, how would we finance it?

The bank offered a first mortgage on the home. In fact, the assistant vice-president remarked, "You guys are already into us for so much money, what's a few more thousand dollars?" But the $22,500 from the bank was still a long way from $52,000.

Then the owner offered to lend the school $15,000 at 5 percent simple interest with fifteen years to pay it off. Wonderful! But that was as far as we could get. We tried every method to borrow the remaining $14,500, but to no avail.

Then I received a phone call on what I considered the last chance to round up the rest of the money, and the answer was *no*. Again, our best human efforts had failed. I hung up the phone, turned to my wife, and said, "I just don't understand the Lord. We're so close, and I know he wants us to have that property, and we just can't get it." No sooner had I said the words than the phone rang again, and the owner's son-in-law, who had an interest in the property himself, had just agreed to give DCS a $10,000 second mortgage on the property. That left only $4,500, which two of us made up ourselves.

I could go on with stories of how our best human efforts have often failed—and how God then stepped in to do what was needed. But I guess my main point is that I believe this school belongs to God. He has showed that to me time and time again.

In starting a Christian school in your area, remember that God is more concerned about the endeavor than you are. Christian education is his concern. Therefore, keeping close contact with him is the most important factor in all your efforts.

For many years, the DCS school board has met often for prayer. Cottage prayer groups have been formed by school families. The school has hosted prayer coffee hours with mothers, and has operated a telephone prayer line with a taped review of current prayer requests. We even have what we call a "perpetual prayer chain" involving our staff, parents, and students. The goal is to saturate our programs and personnel in prayer.

The importance of prayer is so great that it is impossible to state it strongly enough. In a later chapter I'll give more details about how we encourage our families to pray.

In the words of Dr. A. J. Gordon, "You can do more than pray, after you have prayed; but you cannot do more than pray until you have prayed."[2]

5
How Different Should It Be?

STUDENTS FROM CHRISTIAN SCHOOLS consistently rank high in standardized testing. Compared with the woeful cries from public school administrators about graduating students who cannot handle basic reading and math skills, the academic picture among Christian schools is generally well above average, and in some cases, superior.

For instance, for the school year of 1976–77, elementary students in the Western Association of Christian Schools (WACS) ranked from seven to ten months above the national average in grades one to seven and in eighth grade a whopping thirteen months above the national average.[1] WACS high school students (grades nine to twelve), tested in reading, English, and mathematics, also showed a superior grasp of the material.[2]

However, if the Christian school is merely graduating young people who are sharp mentally, we are failing in our most important job. The prophet Jeremiah spoke to Christian parents, administrators, and teachers, as well as to the people of his own day, when he cried, "Let not the wise and skillful person glory and boast in his wisdom and skill . . . ; but let him who glories glory in this, that he understands and knows Me (personally and practically, directly discerning and recognizing My character), that I am the Lord Who practices loving-kindness, judgment and righteousness in the earth; for in these things I delight, says the Lord."[3]

I have become greatly concerned over the past months regarding the most vital task facing the Christian school today: the development of the spirit and the character of our young people. Man is made up of three parts: spirit, soul (mind, emotion, will), and body.[4] Unfortunately, most educators' efforts have been directed toward the mind, ignoring the spirit.

As Bill Gothard says in *Character Sketches*, "The great challenge of our day is to grasp the concept of being mighty in spirit, and to see how it differs from being directed by the intellect. . . . In our day we have unknowingly accepted a standard of education which hinders and destroys the potential of being mighty in spirit, and emphasizes the idea that the highest achievement in education is to be guided by intellect."[5]

In most of what we have been taught and most of what we do today, our minds lead, not our spirits. Most of us have been so brainwashed by the god of reason that we find it very difficult to appreciate that the most important thing we can do for our young people (and in fact for ourselves) is to develop the spirit part of us so that it can lead our lives. (See illustration.)

If we can't reason something out, we tend to think it must not be right. Yet God's ways are different from man's.[6] We must develop sensitivity to God's ways and God's thoughts, which come to us through our spirits.

God intended that we know only good. It was the temptation to know the difference between good and evil that led to the original sin[7] and to spiritual death. And one does not discern evil with the mind, but with the spirit.

In the New Testament, believers are instructed to be "well-versed and wise as to what is good,

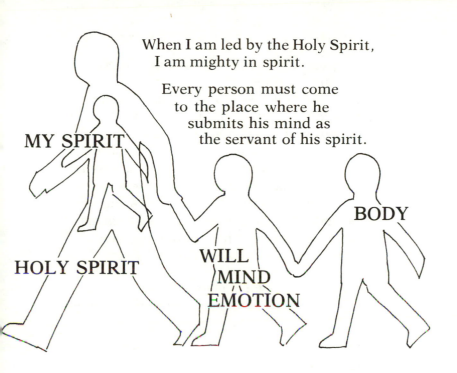

When I am led by the Holy Spirit,
I am mighty in spirit.

Every person must come
to the place where he
submits his mind as
the servant of his spirit.

MY SPIRIT

BODY

HOLY SPIRIT

WILL
MIND
EMOTION

and innocent and guileless as to what is evil."[8]
And evil is not confined to the lists that we have
made; it includes all that is contrary to God's
truth, such as the teaching of evolution or of
situational ethics.

Actually, the idea I am advancing is not new.
Nor is its application confined to students in
Christian schools. It applies to every born-again
believer. It is the same idea that Jesus advanced
when he admonished his followers to "seek
... first the Kingdom of God and his righteousness...."[9]

Paul approached it from yet another angle:
"Whatsoever things are true ... honest ...

just ... pure ... lovely ... of good report ... think on these things."[10]

I was in the business world for seventeen years before becoming superintendent of a Christian school. Much of my time then was spent with computers; so it is easy for me to think of developing a personality, a character, a spirit in terms of data processing. What we allow to come into our lives will find a way of expressing itself, good or bad. "For as [a man] thinks in his heart, so is he."[11] And so will his actions become!

Richard Halverson stated it very well:

"Garbage in ... garbage out!"
It works that way with people as well as computers.

What comes out of a man is *what he puts in*. . .

What he *looks* at. . .

What he *listens* to. . .

What he *reads*. . .

What he *watches*.

His soul is like a *sensitive computer* recording whatever he decides to program in.

The *playback reflects the input* ... and communication to the outside world is on that basis—*often non-verbally*.

Jesus put it this way: "A good man out of the good treasure of the heart bringeth forth good things; and an evil man out of the evil treasure bringeth forth evil things" (Matthew 12:35).

What are you reading? Viewing? What magazines? Books? Movies?

What are you *feeding your soul?*

Nourishing food . . . or garbage?

When you least expect it, what's inside of you will reveal itself, if not by word, . . . by look or action.

"Blessed is the man . . . whose delight is in the law of the Lord and in his law does he meditate day and night" (Psalm 1:2).[12]

It's no wonder that God through Solomon commanded, "Keep your heart with all vigilance and above all that you guard, for out of it flow the springs of life."[13]

I am a product of the secular world. My elementary, high school, and college years were all spent in secular schools. Consequently, I find that I have had a lot of deprogramming to do because in my formal education I was never taught to do things God's way.

Harry Blemires states: "There is no longer a Christian mind . . . the modern Christian has succumbed to secularization. He accepts religion—its morality, its worship, its spiritual culture; but he rejects the religious view of life, the view which sets all earthly issues within the context of the eternal, the view which relates all human problems—social, political, cultural—to the doctrinal foundations of the Christian faith, the view which sees all things here below in terms of God's supremacy and earth's transitoriness, in terms of heaven and hell."[14]

I learned very thoroughly to look at life from man's point of view. Most of us fit into this category. Yet in spite of having been taught that I can handle anything with my mind, I have found that there are some things I just *cannot* watch, some things I *cannot* allow myself to read, some things I *cannot* listen to. Why? Because they will influence me away from God. They will quench the Holy Spirit within me and allow my natural mind, not my redeemed spirit, to control my attitudes and actions. And I will *act* the way I have been taught to *think*. We are to have the mind of Christ; we are to think like him (Philippians 2:5).

One of my favorite stories involves a mother who was preparing a salad for her family. As she scraped the carrots and discarded the outer leaves of the lettuce, her daughter came into the kitchen and asked permission to go to a questionable place of entertainment.

Her mother asked, "Do you really think you should go to a place like that?"

The daughter confidently answered, "I can handle it, Mom. My friends are going too. We won't do anything bad. We just want to see what it's like."

Instead of answering, the mother picked up some of the scraps she had discarded and began mixing them into the salad.

The daughter looked on, horrified. "Mother!" she cried. "You're ruining the salad!"

The mother looked at her daughter and said, "Well, I just figured if you didn't mind putting garbage into your mind, you wouldn't mind putting a little into your stomach."

When it comes to education, *The Living Bible* paraphrase of Proverbs 19:27 instructs us: "Stop listening to teaching that contradicts what you know is right." Most young people are not even able to distinguish what is wrong; thus it becomes a parental responsibility. Christian schools are an invaluable help to parents in this responsibility.

Good is not contagious. Evil is. Like it or not, that's a fact of life in this world. Put one rotten apple in with some good ones. Does it become good? No, the others become rotten. Let a healthy person walk around among sick people. Do they become well just because of his presence? No, but if they have an infectious disease, he will likely become ill.

The Living Bible paraphrase of Haggai 2:11-13 says, "Ask the priests this question about the law: 'If one of you is carrying a holy sacrifice in his robes, and happens to brush against some bread or wine or meat, will it too become holy?'

" 'No,' the priests replied. 'Holiness does not pass to other things that way.'

"Then Haggai asked, 'But if someone touches a dead person, and so becomes ceremonially impure, and then brushes against something, does it become contaminated?'

"And the priests answered, 'Yes,' "

In the *Amplified Bible* that passage ends with the words, "Unholiness is infectious"—another argument against expecting a youngster to withstand the pressures and witness in the public school. He will likely be brought down to his peers' level.

In guarding our affections against that which is unholy, we adults must lead the way.

The more I think along these lines, the more I am forced to examine some of the practices in our school to try to find ways of changing them so that our students will be aided in developing spiritually and in character. Everything we do should aid in developing students into the likeness of Jesus, to think like him and to act like him.

One of the experiences that jarred me into this realization occurred one day when a high school girl stopped me in the hall. She said, "This is a Christian school, but I'm confused. I read my Bible every day, pray privately every day. I really try to obey the Lord; but I've never been chosen for *anything.*"

It was as if she had put a knife in my ribs and twisted it.

Her words caused me to face the fact that even in our Christian school, a lot of what we do is based only on *man's tradition*, not on God's way of doing things. (There's that contrast again!)

Mr. Halverson underscores this contrast:

From God's point of view, to be great—one must *become a servant*...
To be exalted, one must *humble himself*...
To receive—one must *give*...
To be happy—one must *mourn*...
To seek one's life—one must *lose it*...
To lose one's life—is to *find it*.
From the *human standpoint* this is crazy...
But it is *the way of wisdom*. The weariness, the jadedness, the boredom of our contemporary culture testifies to the futility, the emptiness of worldly ways.[15]

Worldly ways...tradition...allowing the mind to lead the spirit instead of the reverse. I fear that we are often guilty of this offense in Christian schools. For instance, we have homecoming festivities every fall. Do you know how we select the homecoming court, the king and queen? It's largely a popularity contest. The students who are the flashiest, the most attractive, the ones with the best personalities: those students are the ones honored.

Traditionally that's the way most schools do it. But what effect does this practice have? It encourages the students to judge by outward appearances. It encourages them to compare themselves with one another. It doesn't help them to become like Jesus.

As a school following this "tradition," we are helping establish the climate for them to feel that God didn't put them together as well as he put someone else together. As a result, many youngsters must wrestle with their self-concepts because they feel inferior to someone else.

Our student council advisor presented this truth to the student council this fall. Afterwards they voted almost unanimously to change our way of handling homecoming activities. Their response was a surprise because, frankly, we had expected the students to resent our suggestion that having the homecoming court was hindering some students in spiritual growth. But instead of resenting the suggestion, they agreed with us! In a later chapter I will describe how the students decided to handle this matter.

Another area that I am praying much about, but don't have a complete answer on yet, is the grading system. We use A, B, C, etc. But again, doesn't that compare Johnny with someone else who has different potential? Our goal is to help each student to become strong in spirit so that he can become effective in the area in which God has called him to serve. Marking his permanent record with our evaluation of his work based on an absolute standard of "average intelligence" doesn't encourage the bright ones to strive harder. And it often discourages the slower ones. It distresses me to see a student who has worked really hard go home with a C, while his brother may have dawdled and still received an A because he was born with a superior mind. We are in the process of changing our report system at the elementary level in grades kindergarten through third to show how Johnny is doing in completing certain objectives academically and with well-defined Christlike character qualities. This will not be in comparison with anyone else.

Our sports program is another area in which we are trying to bring our practices more in line with God's way of doing things. Instead of awarding recognition to a "best offensive player," "best defensive player," etc., we are establishing awards based on positive character qualities such as endurance, diligence, and cooperation.

We are seeing results as young people realize that those with dedication and determination, not just the naturally gifted athletes, will be recognized.

At the Institute for Athletic Perfection we have found some helpful ideas for use in our athletic department to help students develop spiritually.[16] Our coaches are encouraging their team members to play as though Jesus Christ were the only fan in the stands. Our students are learning to release themselves totally to play their hardest, to maintain a Christian attitude throughout the game, and then to rejoice, whatever the scoreboard says.

In the high school drama department, our speech teacher has made up a list of twenty-one positive character qualities that young people can develop by being involved in dramatic productions. The list of qualities include diligence, endurance, discernment, flexibility, orderliness, self-control, resourcefulness. These make up her guideline in working with her students in preparing productions.[17]

In this next area some educators are sure to take issue with me; but we are making some changes in our curriculum. In the past we have chosen textbooks on the basis of which ones would do the best job of developing a youngster's intellect. Now, however, we have begun to implement Christian textbooks as best we can throughout our system.

I am convinced that it is easier for a teacher to add the academic excellence to a textbook, if necessary, than to add God's eternal perspective.

I'd rather risk academic excellence than lose the opportunity to use subject matter to make a student aware of the spiritual significance of his studies.

John C. Whitcomb put it well in his foreword to *Education for the Real World:* "If a study in the realm of liberal arts (whether it be literature, history, philosophy, psychology, biology, or music) does not directly or indirectly support God's special revelation to mankind in the Bible, it must be either drastically revised or dropped. Such surgery in the academic body may be painful, but it is essential for the sake of its spiritual survival."[18]

Next, in trying to bring our financial structure in line with the way we felt God wanted it done, we made a major change in 1971 when we adopted a faith policy. Briefly stated, this policy prevents us from soliciting donations or having fund-raising drives as a school. Needs are made known to those on our mailing list, and we ask God to touch the hearts of those whom he wants to participate in the support of the school. Our students are aware of the policy, and many of them assume a serious sense of responsibility in helping us pray that God will bring in the necessary funds for salaries, mortgage payments, and other expenses. There is no attempt, however, to impose this position on our parents, realizing that God is working differently in different lives. "Grass-root-level" efforts are permitted; that is, groups of parents or friends may sponsor events to interest others in supporting the work here.

While we would not say that other Christian schools should follow the same path, we do praise God that since this policy has gone into operation we have grown from 380 students to 1,495 and from an annual budget of $340,000 to our present one of $1.4 million. God has been gracious to us, particularly considering that our tuition and fees cover only about 85 percent of our expenses. We feel that this financial policy is helping all of us develop spiritually.

The most vital area of concern for any Christian school is its teachers. A school must depend on its teachers more than on anyone else to carry out its philosophy of education, because they are in personal contact with the students in learning situations every school day. No matter how effective the administrators, if the teachers are not in harmony with the school's philosophy, the students will be unreached.

Often school boards evaluate teachers merely according to their academic credentials—the kind of degrees they have. They fail to take a really close look at their spiritual qualifications. Jay Adams in his book, *The Big Umbrella*, declares that for a teacher "holiness of life must be a prime qualification." He suggests that a teacher have the attitude: "My qualifications must extend beyond an academic degree. Qualifications must extend to my quality of life. I must become the right kind of person before I am qualified to teach. When I am right in God's sight, then I shall be right to stand before his children. . . ."[19]

With this truth in mind, we have made up a unique teacher application. On it are seven situations in which a teacher might find himself. For instance, the applicant is asked what his response would be if another teacher came to his room and began to criticize the principal. And what if a student came to him and said something derogatory about another teacher?

By studying answers to these and other hypothetical situations, we are able to sense whether the teacher has a biblical approach to life. No one ever scores 100 percent. We don't expect that. But having a potential teacher indicate his response gives us a chance to go over the

Bible pattern (in the cases above, Matthew 18:15-17). And if the teacher is hired, he knows what we expect in some of the experiences he might face.

Some other questions we ask:

Tell about your family background, your upbringing.

What do you feel your response should be to authority?

What do you think are your strengths as a teacher?

Your weaknesses?

What do you like about yourself?

Dislike?

What have you learned recently from your personal study of the Word of God?

Is Christian education a conviction or just a preference for you?

Are you in debt?

If the applicant is single, we ask: How does your family feel about your working here? How does your father feel?

What do you think about marriage?

Are you willing to live a single life if God calls you to do that?

If the candidate is married, we insist on interviewing the partner. This practice helps minimize later conflicts that may arise if the husband or wife does not understand the requirements of working at our school. It also helps get the marriage partner "on our team" because he/she knows we consider him/her to be important.

If we are really interested in a teacher candidate, we arrange for him to spend an evening socially with one of our board members and his

family. It is important to see if he is on the same "wave length" as we are, if he has attitudes that harmonize with our school's approach.

I find myself frequently referring to the subject of teachers because I cannot overemphasize their importance in developing students who are strong in spirit and pure in character. (See illustration.) But for now in considering how different a teacher in a Christian school should be, let me suggest that he be as well qualified academically as possible, but even more important, that he be a committed believer who wants to grow in obedience, one who senses that God wants him in a Christian school to help develop the next generation in spirit and in character.

6
Making It Workable

IN DEVELOPING THE SPIRIT & CHARACTER of ourselves and of our youth, it is basic to become conscious of God in every circumstance, every time, and every place. God-consciousness involves a constant awareness of him, with the goal of allowing him to determine our every thought, word, decision, action. It is seeing all of life from the eyes of Jesus. The classic little book, *The Practice of the Presence of God*, urges ". . . that we might accustom ourselves to a continual conversation with him with freedom and simplicity, that we need only to recognize God intimately present with us, to address ourselves to him every moment."[1]

That is surely the ultimate in God-consciousness. How does one attain such a state?

To begin with, I would like to refer to the experience of a modern saint who is respected internationally: Corrie ten Boom. When Corrie was separated from all her loved ones, stripped of all her possessions, cast into solitary confinement in prison, she found that her most precious comfort was the presence of God. God in her! The presence of the Holy Spirit was her dearest treasure because no force could take it away from her.

What she learned in the extremity of her suffering, we can begin to learn even now: that each of us as a believer is a living temple for the Spirit of God.

Again I refer to *The Practice of the Presence of God*, a collection of conversations held with a modest monk who worked in the kitchen of a seventeenth-century monastery. In it the author recounts Brother Lawrence as feeling that "it was a great delusion to think that the times of prayer ought to differ from other times. . . . We should find that when the appointed times of prayer are past, we find no difference because we continue with God, praising and blessing him with all our might."[2]

Of himself, the monk confessed, "The time of business does not with me differ from the time of prayer, and in the noise and clatter of my kitchen, while several persons are at the same time calling for different things, I possess God in as great tranquility as if I were upon my knees at the blessed sacrament."[3]

Being conscious of someone's physical presence is a common experience with us. My wife and I often sit in the family room at home, reading and not saying a word to each other for thirty or forty minutes; but if something comes to my mind that I want to say to her, I speak immediately. She does the same with me. That's the way we are to walk with God: aware of his presence, ready to ask, "Jesus, what do you want me to do in this situation?" or "Jesus, I need help with a problem."

I am not speaking of a state of perfection, but a matter of direction. Becoming truly God-conscious and communing with him is the work of a lifetime; yet we can begin to move in that direction this very moment. For young people, developing this awareness of God's presence, developing a biblical view of life, is facilitated by a Christian school in which Jesus and his Word are central to all its activities.

I've had students come to me and say they won't become Christians because they see too many hypocrites. I say, "You're right; hypocrites are numerous. I'm a hypocrite too. But I like to think that every day of my life I'm less a hypocrite than I was the day before."

We all wear facades with each other. Our kids sense this and reject it. But when we come to a place of honestly saying, "I'm going to direct my attention, my energies, to living this moment in an awareness of the presence of God," a power is released in our lives. Our kids will sense that too.

A few years ago I was asked to be a staff member at the National Institute for Christian School Administrators, sponsored by Grace College and National Christian School Education Association (now part of the Association of Christian Schools International). When I found that not only was I giving workshops to small groups, but I was to speak at one of the general sessions, I was petrified. Many of those on staff and in attendance were people I looked up to, people who had had an important ministry in giving me insights and direction for my efforts at our school. Now all of a sudden I was to stand up before them? I was just about frightened to death. And to make matters worse, it was not until Thursday morning that I would speak to the general session, so I had all week to think about it and get still more nervous.

The room in which I was staying that week "just happened" to have a plaque on the wall. I didn't see plaques in any other rooms in that building. The Scripture verse on that plaque was Isaiah 26:3: "Thou wilt keep him in perfect peace, whose mind is stayed on thee: because he trusteth in thee."

I went to bed with that verse in mind, and I got

up to that verse. As the week went on and I meditated on that truth, I became calmer and calmer because I realized that the Spirit of God was within me. As I opened my mind to think upon him, his promise was that I would have perfect peace. And I did.

I began to realize that all I was going to do in that general session was to stand where he wanted me to stand. You know, there never need be a struggle for Christians. We are to rest in him, abide in him. Let him take our minds, our mouths, our bodies. . . so that what is said and done is his responsibility. All he asks for is a prepared and yielded vessel.

S. D. Gordon defined God-consciousness like this: "Jesus walking around in my shoes, expressing himself through my lips and my presence."

On a flight to the East Coast to speak at the Mid-Atlantic Christian School Convention, I had with me my son, who was at that time a sixth grader. We knew that at ten o'clock that morning my wife was going to visit a sick woman and share the gospel with her, so at that hour we bowed our heads and asked God to give her the words to say to express the Lord Jesus to that woman. As I closed the prayer, I said, "Lord, we really love you and we really desire to please you. Amen."

My son looked at me and asked, "Dad, how can I really love someone I can't see?"

What he actually wanted to know was, "How can I get to know Jesus like I know you?"

To most young people, having a personal relationship implies that when they speak, the other person answers audibly; or if they write, he will write back. Most youngsters' picture of Jesus is of a man who came into the world 2,000 years ago, lived thirty-three years, died on a cross, rose from the dead, and is going to come back in the future; but they don't know Jesus in the *now*. They don't know that he is alive, a Person they can speak to, a Person who can speak to them from his Word.

Knowing Jesus personally is different from knowing someone else, because Jesus doesn't behave like a flesh-and-blood person. He doesn't write letters; he doesn't call us on the telephone; he doesn't say "hi" to us. Jesus does not communicate with us in the way that we do with one another; yet he *does communicate* with us. And it is not in a "second best" fashion. No place in the book of Acts did the disciples long for the "good old days" when they walked side by side with Jesus, because they had something even better: a daily awareness of the risen Lord in the *now* of their lives.

The Lord Jesus does not communicate with us like a human person for the reason that he is a *Spirit Person*. John 4:24 says, "God is a Spirit: and they that worship him must worship him in spirit and in truth."

We must teach ourselves, as well as our young people, how to develop this spirit relationship with the Lord Jesus, how to worship him in spirit and in truth.

To begin with, we learn to communicate with him in the spirit by feeding on his Word. Jeremiah 15:16 says, "Thy words were found, and I did eat them; and thy word was unto me the joy and rejoicing of mine heart. . . ." Psalm 103:20 says, "Bless the Lord, ye his angels, that excel in strength, that do his commandments, hearkening unto the voice of his word." To be filled with God's Word is to be filled with his voice. He speaks his Word to us. The Word is our food and drink; yet many Christians are starving!

I encourage our faculty and student body to read thcough the Bible every year. We have made charts available to them so that they can keep a record as they are reading through the Scriptures. For those who feel they cannot accomplish the readings in a year, we encourage them to do it systematically and take two or three years. We just challenge them to read the Word of God every day!

Often my Bible reading for the morning gives me new insights into my students' needs. I share with the students and teachers what I have learned in my personal devotions.

To learn to communicate with Jesus in the spirit requires that we follow our reading with *memorizing* of Scripture. Colossians 3:16 tells us, "Let the word of Christ dwell in you richly. . . ." In the Old Testament, Egypt's seven years of plenty were followed by several years of famine. During the prosperity they were told to store up in preparation for the famine (Genesis 41). We are living today in spiritual prosperity, and we should be storing up God's Word. Strong memory programs are vital to our homes, churches, and schools, and should have priority attention.

In our school we have an ambitious Scripture memorization program. For grades kindergarten through six we use the Bible Memory Association books, and until this year in our junior high and high school we have had weekly recitations on programs which corresponded with each grade's Bible study. This year all of our junior and senior high students are studying positive character qualities and reciting memory verses which illustrate them. (See sample page of character qualities memory verse work.)

I believe it is very important that we teachers and administrators also memorize Scripture. I teach a class of seniors and have told them that if I cannot recite the verses on recitation day, they will not have to do theirs either. They have the right to call me on the carpet that day and have me recite for them.

It is important that we set the example for this quality of living that we are teaching. If it is really true, then *we* had better be doing it! The same applies to parents who want to see their children grow spiritually. They had better be careful to practice what they urge their youngsters to do!

Meditation should follow the memorization of God's Word (1 Timothy 4:15, 16). Meditation is a forgotten art in our day, and who but God can measure the loss to the Christian world! Ruminate (bring to mind and consider again and again), ponder the Word—this is meditation! One must hear, read, study, and memorize God's Word—but then one must meditate on it!

Scripture records many promises to persons who memorize and meditate on Scripture. The promises include success (Joshua 1:8), prosperity (Psalm 1:1-3), understanding (Psalm 119:99), new power over sin (Psalm 119:9-11), joy (Psalm

63:5, 6), peace (Psalm 119:165), faith (Romans 10:17), wisdom (Psalm 119:98), and success that is obvious to all (1 Timothy 4:15).

As a parent, these blessings are far more important to me than intellectual achievement, for they last into eternity. This, of course, is not to minimize academic accomplishment, but to bring it into proper spiritual perspective.

In my personal meditation, I have frequently pondered Proverbs 16:3: "Commit thy works unto the Lord, and thy thoughts shall be established." This verse tells me that if I give to the Lord my day's responsibilities as a husband, father, and school administrator, God will then program my mind to get me through it step by step—to do just exactly what he wants done that day. Having come from the computer world, I can easily envision a program laid out step by step, minutely detailed. Such a program would cause me to carry out my responsibilities for that day. When I finish that day, I can rest assured that what has been accomplished was exactly what God wanted—no more and no less. Meditating on that verse has given me that kind of assurance!

Another way to encourage youngsters to know Jesus is by helping them learn to share their faith with others. This is often best done by sharing the overflow of your own experiences in witnessing.

I have made a personal commitment to the Lord that not one salesman will come into my office without my sharing Jesus with him. Sometimes I fail to live up to this commitment; but several times I have had the joy of leading some-

LOVE Due 3/2
Giving to others' basic needs without
having as my motive personal reward.

I Corinthians 13:3
And though I bestow all my goods to feed the poor, and
though I give my body to be burned, and have not charity, it
profiteth me nothing.

Romans 12:9, 10
Let love be without *dissimulation. Abhor that which is
evil; cleave to that which is good. Be kindly affectioned one
to another with brotherly love; in honor preferring one
another.
　*Dissimulation - hypocrisy

Romans 13:10
Love worketh no ill to his neighbor: therefore love is the
fulfilling of the law.

LOYALTY Due 3/9
Using adversity to confirm my commitment
to those whom God has called me to serve.

John 15:13
Greater love hath no man than this, that a man lay down his
life for his friends.

Proverbs 17:9
He that covereth a transgression seeketh love; but he that
repeateth a matter separateth very friends.

Proverbs 25:19
Confidence in an unfaithful man in time of trouble is like a
broken tooth, and a foot out of joint.

one to faith. For instance, the insurance salesman who has our annuity program received
Christ in my office. So did the man who handled
our health and major medical program in the
past. That particular man was late for our ap-
pointment. He was due at 2:00 P.M. and did not
arrive until 2:40. I had another meeting
scheduled at 2:45, and people were waiting outside my office for it. I wanted to sign his papers

73

and get him out of my office; but God impressed on me that I had to share Christ with him right then.

I went out to the people and told them to go to the library across the hall, and that I would be with them later. I am thankful I did, because that man prayed and received Christ that afternoon.

Giving special attention to spiritual matters for a full day helps develop a relationship with Jesus also. We have four days of spiritual emphasis, one for each grading period. During these days we forget textbooks and normal classroom schedules. Instead we begin the day with a special speaker or a Christian film. Then we have electives at the junior high and high school level. We offer subjects such as dating, the occult, music, authority, missions—any topic of interest; and we examine it from a biblical viewpoint. At the end of the day we have a praise service.

Once I taught a class on the subject of life after death. I taught three sessions that day. We talked about heaven, about hell. At the end of the day a senior boy came forward and received Christ. He said he had never thought in total about what happens after death. The day was a turning point in his life.

Another way to make Jesus real is to emphasize talking to him. We use many methods to make our students and our school families conscious of the importance of prayer. Prayer is sensing God's presence moment by moment, and we would like for prayer to permeate our school atmosphere.

We have developed a perpetual prayer chain for two weekends a year. Starting Friday at 6 P.M.

and going through the next Monday morning, we have parents, students, and faculty members take fifteen-minute periods and pray for the ministry of the school.

We use prayer request forms that devotional teachers fill out at the beginning of the day. These are brought to the office and assembled and posted so that everyone can know what we are currently praying about. Also they are often put on our twenty-four-hour telephone prayer line. This telephone tape helps keep open communication within our school family, because we don't have a chance to assemble on Sundays or Wednesdays, as a church does.

Classroom prayer is important, but it doesn't have to occur at the beginning of the period. Sometimes it is good to close a class with prayer. Sometimes stopping in the middle of class, especially if there is some problem, is a practical reminder that God is always present and ready to hear our voices. We also have a prayer chapel, and we allow students to go from study halls to use this chapel.

Besides our regular faculty devotions before school every morning, we periodically make provision for the students to gather for prayer before school. A teacher is excused from faculty devotions to meet with any students who voluntarily come to a designated room. At lunchtime a room is also designated with a teacher present. Those who wish may come there, eat their lunches, sing, and pray together, as they wish.

One morning a month, each principal has a prayer coffee for parents. With school families divided geographically, we have cottage prayer meetings in homes in each area. So far there have not been big crowds responding to these meetings; but God has blessed even when only a few came. And our school has been helped by the prayers that were offered.

From another Christian school we borrowed an idea for a praise and prayer booklet in which we have a page for each day of the month. For each day we have a praise item, a prayer request, and the names of specific faculty members we want our school family to pray for that day. (Sample page enclosed.)

Finally, another borrowed idea is that of the "Fanner Bee" program. I am told that fanner bees, which are no longer able to gather honey, fan their wings and thus keep the temperature constant and the air in the beehive sweet. Without their work, the hive would die. So we seek out older people to pray for our students. Ideally, we will assign one student to each older person until all the students in our school are covered. This program is still in its beginning stages, but I can see great potential for the prayers of older saints to bless our young people.

Everything I have said so far in this chapter can be done; yet a young person might still be completely turned off to the idea of God-consciousness without one last vital area: *a life of praise.* Christian schools should be full of rejoicing people. Frankly, I'm tired of seeing believers walking around with their shoulders low, looking as if the world is coming in on them. As I read the Scriptures, I find that it tells us to rejoice *always.* And it says we are to give praise *in all things.*

13th DAY OF THE MONTH

Promise: "Now unto him that is able to do exceeding abundantly above all that we ask or think according to the power that worketh in us." Ephesians 3:20

Praise God for the privilege of Christian fellowship.

Pray for our Social Studies teachers: Lee Reno, Gary McDowell, Phil Hayes, Ruth Risser.

14th DAY OF THE MONTH

Promise: "Humble yourselves in the sight of the Lord, and he shall lift you up." James 4:10

Praise God for the people who regularly help with building maintenance.

Pray for our Math teachers: Alan Arment, Mike Buck, Helen Miller, Roger Wilson.

15th DAY OF THE MONTH

Promise: "Casting all your care upon him; for he careth for you." 1 Peter 5:7

Praise God for the unity of the staff of Dayton Christian Schools.

Pray for our Science teachers: Lloyd Davis, Steve Karnehm, Tom Minor, Ron Pinsenschaum.

16th DAY OF THE MONTH

Promise: "Evening and morning, and at noon, will I pray, and cry aloud: and he shall hear my voice." Psalm 55:17

Praise God for the faculty he has brought together.

Pray for our Language Arts teachers: English: Bob Clements, Arline Jackson, Faith King, Susie Neal, Sally Ott, Paul Pyle, Carole Reeves. French: Faith King. Spanish: Susana Wyatt. Speech/Drama: Ruth Clements.

17th DAY OF THE MONTH

Promise: "If we confess our sins, he is faithful and just to forgive us our sins, and to cleanse us from all unrighteousness." 1 John 1:9

Praise God for his faithfulness in supplying our financial needs.

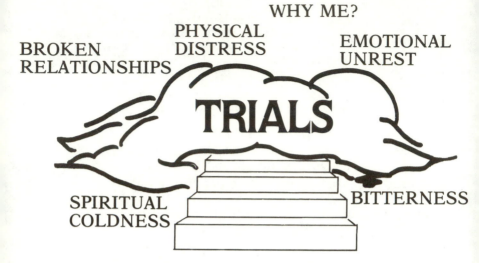

WHY ME?

PHYSICAL DISTRESS

EMOTIONAL UNREST

BROKEN RELATIONSHIPS

TRIALS

SPIRITUAL COLDNESS

BITTERNESS

Normally when we face a trial in our school or in our personal lives, we begin to say, "Why me, God? What did I do to deserve this?" (See illustration.) Though those words may not actually come out of our mouths, we show that spirit in the way we look. Then, before we know it, relationships are broken, and spiritual coldness or bitterness sets in. Too many Christian schoolteachers and administrators are bitter. If we are bitter, it is going to affect every area of our lives. We had better get it resolved fast.

When we go through a trial, we must remind ourselves that there will be an end to it. And when we come out of it, we are meant to come forth as gold.[4] God is sovereign. Nothing comes into our lives without his loving permission, so we can confidently thank him in all things. (See illustration.)

GOD IS ALWAYS RIGHT!

VICTORY!

PRAISE GOD!

TRIALS

THANK YOU, JESUS!

SEEING JESUS!

Some time ago I was driving to a meeting of the Ohio Association of Christian Schools. Since the meeting was in the northern part of the state, I left very early in the morning. I had just gotten a new car and it had cruise control. So when I got on the highway, I accelerated to about fifty-five miles an hour and pushed the cruise control button. Then I sat back and just steered, because there was really no traffic on the road.

After a while I noticed a patrol car parked on the median strip ahead. Knowing that he was there as a radar trap, I glanced at my speedometer just to make sure I was still at fifty-five. Yes, I was within the speed limit. But just as I got up to him, his red light started flashing. I wondered who he was after. Then I realized he was after *me!* When he pulled me over to the side, I asked, "Officer, what have I done?"

He said, "You were speeding."

"Officer, you've got to be kidding. I've got cruise control on this car, and I was going fifty-five."

"No, I clocked you at sixty-six miles an hour."

He took me back to his cruiser; there was his radar blinking "66."

I said, "This just can't be." But suddenly God reminded me to give thanks in all things.[5] I said to myself, "Thank You, Jesus."

I really didn't understand why God let it happen; but then I thought maybe he wanted me to share Christ with that patrolman. So when he gave me a ticket, I said, "I've got something to share with you." I gave him a tract and talked with him about the Lord. No, he didn't receive Christ right then, but I have to believe that our meeting was not by accident.

Later that month I had to go to court. Meanwhile, I had taken my car back to the dealer and found that the speedometer was out of calibration. When it read fifty-five, I was really going sixty-six.

I was to be at court at 9 A.M., and I really hated to be away from the school. What made it even worse, it was 11:30 before I was called before the judge.

But in that two and one-half hours, did I get a picture of the depravity of man and what's really going on today in the lives of people! It was unreal. The domestic squabbles! The selfishness and sin! God used that exposure to awaken me to the need to go back to school with a new vigor and teach our students even more diligently about the right way to live.

To end the story, the judge threw out the ticket because I had evidence that I was really not trying to violate the law.

By the way, I shared that experience with our students, not to pat myself on the back, but to illustrate the principle of praising God, because when I began to praise God, all of a sudden the burden was released. No longer was I frustrated and upset. I realized that God was in control. We need to demonstrate to our students our faith in that fact because our youngsters are going to face frustrating situations and they need to see that praise *works!*

Another factor that turns young people away from our message of God-consciousness is a spirit of disunity among Christians. Jesus prayed that all his followers would be one, so that the world might believe that the Father had sent him.[6] In fact, he said that the way the world will know that we are his disciples is through our love for one another.[7]

Sherwood Wirt, editor emeritus of *Decision* magazine, expressed his concern about this problem in these words: "My hope is that there will be a revival of love for each other among Christians. I see no other way for evangelicals to avoid becoming big, pompous and proud. As long as others see us fighting, they want no part of us."[8]

I am grieved to see the division among groups of Christians today. It is vital that there be an atmosphere of love and respect for one another if we are to exemplify Christlike love. I am not suggesting that we compromise those issues that sometimes divide us. I am advancing the notion that we *stress* those central doctrines that as born-again Christians we all *agree on.*

How I praise God for our school. He has blessed us with a truly interdenominational staff and faculty. Several different denominations are represented among us; yet we have sweet fellowship in prayer and sharing each school morning. Together we work to lead our students to see that Jesus Christ and the Bible are central to any successful believer's life.

People shake their heads when they hear about the unity we enjoy. It is unique that I can be at a Baptist church one Sunday to receive a check for our school from their missionary budget; and the next Sunday I may be at an Assemblies of God church to receive their support.

I honestly feel that this is the kind of unity God wants. In no area is anyone compromising what he believes, but each one has his eyes focused upon Jesus. There is a oneness as we live and work together in honest and mutual love.

Yet that unity must be carefully guarded. How Satan would love to insert misunderstanding, suspicion, and hurt feelings. By doing so, he would tear us apart.

Whenever I sense a lack of unity with a brother believer, I ask myself, "Have I done something to offend him?" If so, it is my responsibility to go to that person and ask his forgiveness.

Some time ago I became concerned about a barrier that had come between me and a pastor in our area. I struggled with it, and I always came up with the conclusion, "He's all wrong. He's anti-Christian-school." (And he was.) But I never had any peace. As I thought and prayed about it, suddenly God showed me that the barrier was my fault. The problem resulted from a sense of pride in my own life. I'm a very opinionated person; whenever something went well in our school, I couldn't wait to say, "See, I told you so. Christian schools are right."

So one day I went unannounced and asked to see him. I said, "We are brothers in Christ, and I have come to realize that I have been wrong in my attitude toward you. Will you forgive me?"

We talked for an hour. The barrier was gone. He didn't change his attitude toward Christian schools much, but there was once again a unity between us as brother believers. And that was worth more than my pride.

In every home, every church, every school, there are a multitude of interpersonal relationships. If Satan can cut off any line of communication, he will achieve a victory. In a great many Christian groups today, that's exactly what's happening. What people end up with then is gossip and slander that counter their works. In such an atmosphere, it's impossible to enjoy the blessed presence of God or to teach students to do so.

Giving bad reports. Talking about someone behind his back. Saying something negative about a teacher, a parent, a student, an administrator. Such carelessness is today hindering and even destroying many works of God.

For this reason the administrators and faculty in our system spent one weekend on a retreat discussing how we could handle such a threat. It was not yet a problem, but we felt that the larger we grew, the easier it would be for such a problem to arise.

The results have been beautiful in my life personally and in the life of our school.

The principle we studied is outlined in Matthew 18:15-17: "Moreover if thy brother shall trespass against thee, go and tell him his fault between thee and him alone: if he shall hear thee, thou hast gained thy brother. But if he will not hear thee, then take with thee one or two more, that in the mouth of two or three witnesses every word may be established. And if he shall neglect to hear them, tell it unto the church: but if he neglect to hear the church, let him be unto thee as an heathen man and a publican."

This principle of interpersonal relationships will cause gossip to cease in a group. It will also cause Christians to edify each other.

"A whisperer separateth chief friends."[9] Gossip destroys friendships. It builds insecurity and suspicion within groups. But if we will practice love honestly, we will edify one another, build one another up.

Love builds security and a sense of loyalty. It is a comfort to me to know that as chief administrator of our school, my teachers have committed themselves not to give a bad report about me. They know that if they have a complaint about any of my actions, my door is open. I *want* them to come to me personally. I believe it is a comfort to them to know that I will not give a bad report about them.

When a parent calls me to give a bad report about a teacher, I cut him off as nicely as I can and ask, "Have you talked to that teacher?" If he says, "No, I haven't," I say, "Then you must go to that teacher first. If you're not satisfied about the matter, I'll be glad to go with you as a witness."

Since I began following this practice, I have had only one parent come back to me. In every other case the matter has been settled between the teacher and the parent without my being involved!

God's ways are always right. They make sense; they work. And by our "loving honestly," the world will believe that Jesus is who he said he was. Our unity will be a witness of his power.

As helpful reminders, we are using an idea developed by the chairman of our Bible department. It is a little cardboard sign which we place on our desks. It says G R E A T, which stands for "*G*ood *R*eports *E*dify *a*nd *T*estify."

These are made to stand up so that the sign faces two ways. Someone sitting on the other side of my desk sees G R E A T, and on my side of the desk I also see G R E A T. Thus we are reminded of the goal of always giving a good report, never a bad report, about someone else. (See illustration.)

By the way, when we approach someone with whom we have a difference, we are to do it in love, in the spirit of Galatians 6:1: "Brethren, if a man be overtaken in a fault, ye which are spiritual, restore such an one in the spirit of meekness; considering thyself, lest thou also be tempted."

In going to a brother, we seek to restore, not accuse. That is another part of "loving honestly."

An interesting by-product of this matter of

committing ourselves to good reports is that when our teachers are asked to fill out references for students for college admission or for job applications, the teacher will sit down with the student and go over the form with him if it is necessary to report anything negative. And, though it is quite a step of faith, when we send out letters asking for references on our teacher candidates, we ask the person not to give us any negative report about the candidate unless he has first pointed out the problem to the candidate. That is a hard step for us to take naturally, because we want to know if there is a problem in this person we may hire; but we feel that it is consistent with the spirit of Matthew 18.

Finally, we come to the crucial matter of the Christian home. With the divorce rate soaring and with so few truly happy marriages today, we feel a responsibility to do what we can to help our school families strengthen their homes.

Beginning with our school board, we are committed to having only one evening meeting a month. We want our school board members to have time with their families; so if we need other meetings, we make them on Saturday mornings, quite early. We're usually back home with our families by 9:00 or 9:30 A.M., about the time the children are getting up.

In regard to teachers, we are becoming convinced that when a woman has elementary age children of her own, she should not be teaching in our school unless her children are in the same building with her. Too long we have rationalized and said that it's all right for a woman to teach

GREAT

Good Reports Edify And Testify

other people's children, when her own may suffer because she is not available to them.

We urge our staff and faculty to put their families first, ahead of the school. Sometimes that hurts. We'd rather not take that position; but we're convinced it is biblical.

Our teachers are instructed to begin parent conferences with something like this: "Our goal in this school is to help you accomplish the job God has given you with your children. What can we do to help you be more effective in rearing your children?"

Normally the parent has some ideas to suggest. Later in the interview he may turn the question around: "What can we as parents do to help you in your work here at school?"

We are particularly impressed that fathers today need help in assuming their place of spiritual leadership. Charles Haddon Spurgeon said, "School masters are well enough; but godly fathers are, both by the order of nature and grace, the best instructors of their sons. Nor can they delegate that sacred duty. When fathers are tongue-tied religiously, need they wonder if their children's hearts remain sin-tied?"[10] We periodically sponsor sessions for our fathers. We also encourage our teachers to contact the dads first for all communication with the home.

Our schools can help the family in many other ways. Let your imagination go: seminars in sex education, financial freedom, husband-wife relationships, parent-child relationships.

Why is all this a part of making God-consciousness workable? Because the young person who benefits most from Christian school training is the one who has a godly home that is reinforcing what is taught at school.

7
It's Working

IN A PREVIOUS CHAPTER I MENTIONED that we have made a change in the way we observe homecoming festivities in our high school. In earlier years we had a king and a queen with their court of young people selected by the student body. Though there was some faculty input, for the most part the selection was a popularity contest.

This year when our student council advisor suggested that such a practice encouraged students to value only the "outside" of another person, the student council agreed. After several weeks of planning, they came up with an alternative.

The students from each high school class who had been nominated for the honor of representing their class in the homecoming celebration were asked to write a two-page testimony of their faith in Jesus Christ and explain how Dayton Christian School had made a difference in their lives. (It took only one vote to be a candidate; and since the nomination was by secret ballot, a student could even vote for him/herself!) These testimonies were posted on a bulletin board in a much-traveled hall of the high school. There the student body was free to examine the contents and make their decisions on the basis of something besides personal charm and appearance. A pastor's reference was also required, to indicate the student's involvement in the activities of his/her respective church. Later the candidates appeared before their respective classes and fielded questions posed by members of the faculty.

When the actual election was completed, the

honored students were called hosts and host-
esses, not king, queen, and court. They were presented at the homecoming soccer game. For the
rest of the school year, when a guest needed to be
escorted through the building or a new student
needed some help, or a prospective parent visited
the school, an appropriate host or hostess took
over and made the visitor or newcomer feel at
home. They also served as an advisory council to
the principal in preparing spiritual emphasis
days and in evaluating chapels.

At the homecoming banquet there was a
"throne" placed prominently in the room and a
place set at the head table for our King, Jesus
Christ. Both the empty throne and the empty
place at the table reminded the students of the
One who is truly King of kings. Also the banquet
programs spelled out the meaning of the symbols
and gave a clear testimony to God's plan of salvation through Jesus Christ.

Of course, I was pleased with the student
council's alternative, especially since it was their
own idea and they approached the project with
so much enthusiasm and originality.

Sometimes students must have the teacher
outline for them the correlation between their
present activities and spiritual truth. In this regard our senior government course has been an
example of a job well done. To begin with, the
biblical perspective of government is investigated. Due to the basic evil in human nature,
man must have government; he cannot fully control himself. The Christian's responsibility to
government is to obey, pray, and pay taxes![1]

In this senior course, each student must choose an elected official and write to him (her), promising to pray for that person during the rest of the calendar year. To make sure the promise is kept, prayer for the officials is held in class at least once a week. The letter must tell why the student is praying and must have some form of witness (a tract enclosed, stationery with a Scripture verse on it, or a testimony of the student's own faith in Christ; whatever the student feels comfortable with). The teacher reads the letters and mails them.

Later in the semester the same class will study current social problems such as abortion, capital punishment, and gun control. Each student will select one problem and research the laws presently governing it and the pros and cons of changes that might be made. Most importantly, he will research biblical principles that apply to the problem. Then he will propose a solution. He will send his proposal to ten officials (two senators, one representative, leaders of the House and Senate, one of the justices, cabinet officers, etc.). In addition, he will write a letter to one of the local newspapers, proposing his solution to the problem. Again, the teacher will look over all the letters himself before mailing them.

Even in the tenth grade the social studies classes tackle current social problems such as family relationships, male and female roles, love, perversion, communal life, proper methods of dissent, body care (health, drugs, diet, fasting), mass media, work ethic, modern art, and music. Approaching these subjects from the perspective of the Scriptures is important in view of all the ungodly opinions that are being flung at young people.

In the language arts department special stress is laid on helping students develop a "biblical sieve," that is, helping them evaluate literature in the light of Scripture. Different world views of the authors are dealt with among the upper classmen; and in book reports the characters are examined for both positive and negative character traits. Of the six books required for outside reading, at least two of them must be Christian biography or Christian fiction.

At the elementary level where students are so open to the teacher's influence, there are many opportunities to integrate spiritual truth with subject matter. With our elementary art teacher, for instance, it amazes me to find that almost every project has a direct spiritual application.

When she has the children draw pictures inside "television sets" depicting their favorite programs, she asks, "Does this program violate any of the Ten Commandments?" Lively discussions cause the children to begin to evaluate their TV entertainment in the light of Scripture.

When the children gather leaves in the fall for various projects, the teacher asks, "What has happened in your lives since the last time the leaves turned colors?" Usually several children report that they have given their hearts to Christ in the last year. Some report that they get along better with a brother or sister. The teacher steers the students to remember and discuss their growth in character or in spirit.

The children love to do their names in bean

mosaics. They are helped to find out the meaning of their names and to make their plaques as attractive as possible. Bean mosaics require patience and diligence. Sometimes students want to give up before the project is completed. This gives the teacher an opportunity to remind them that they are developing important character traits when they keep going in a tedious job. (For those who have really tackled a larger project than they can handle, she has bird seed or rice handy for a quick finish, though!)

Often this year the bulletin boards have stressed the fruit of the Spirit.[2] In fact, the entire South Elementary School has taken one fruit for each month of the school year. There is a concerted effort in the classroom and on the playground to stress the qualities of gentleness, long-suffering, goodness, etc. Many books and materials are available to help teach the importance of the fruit of the Spirit at the elementary level.[3] (Interestingly enough, the teachers and principal chose *self-control* for the last month of school!)

Teachers in Christian schools have more freedom to be creative and innovative than teachers in public schools because nothing is off-limits as long as it is wholesome and helpful to the students.

Often teachers arrange for their classes to take favors to nursing homes or hospitals. Depending on the students' age and preparation, they may sing, hold a service, or just talk with the patients.

In the junior high and high school this year, special projects have included filling "love loaves" for World Vision to help feed the hungry of the world, filling food baskets for local families who are in need, sending pages of the Russian New Testament to Russian Christians (through a program sponsored by Evangelism to Communist Lands),[4] and "adopting" a missionary sister school overseas. In our American culture, so oriented to self-indulgence and personal convenience, action programs such as these help youngsters catch something of the Christian spirit of love and sharing.

These are only a few ideas for integrating spiritual truth with academics, art, and projects. In each locality many avenues of action will present themselves. Christian education gives an opportunity not to shelter students from the excesses of American culture, but to disciple students to a contemporary Christ who demands our best today.

It's working. I'm thankful to God that he is letting me have a part in the action.

8
We Call Them "Miracles"

RECENTLY WE SENT A QUESTIONNAIRE to our alumni. On it we asked them to state what difference (if any) they felt had resulted in their spiritual lives because of their years at Dayton Christian School. One young man who is training for the ministry wrote, "One big difference it has made is that I know what faith can do, faith that looks beyond the balance figure of a budget. DCS runs on faith—faith in God—and that fact made a big difference in my outlook on life."

Reports like that stimulate us to lift our chins and keep on going, even when circumstances look dark.

This young man graduated with a class that lived through one of the most remarkable events in our history: the acquisition of a building for our high school. I would like to tell this story as another illustration of the principle I referred to in an earlier chapter: that God often allows us to reach utter helplessness before he gives the answer to our needs.

In the fall of 1972 it became evident that our fast-growing high school needed another building because its present quarters were too small. (By this time, I had left the business world and become superintendent of the school.)

Though an architect had drawn plans for a building to be erected on acreage next to the elementary campus, the school board members and administrators also began scouting the Dayton area for suitable buildings that might be already available. We investigated every possible lead, evaluating locations, touring buildings, asking questions. Larger facilities for the next school year were essential, and there was no time for us to get a building up that fast. Yet we couldn't find anything suitable on the market.

When the outlook was bleakest, Julienne, a Catholic all-girl high school, announced plans to merge with the local Catholic boys' school; and its lovely wooded campus with 80,000 square feet of facilities was put on the market.* An additional 45,000 square feet were included in the convent next door, where the Sisters of Notre Dame, the controlling order, had lodged its members. The property had been officially appraised at $1.3 million, with $6 million considered the price of reproducing the facilities. Buying this property would make more economic sense than putting up a new building!

During the school year 1972–73, we kept this matter before our faculty and student body, urging them to pray earnestly concerning the facilities. Enthusiasm was high as we negotiated to buy the beautiful Julienne property. Certain that God would give us that building, we openly shared our confidence with the student body.

Then suddenly it was announced in the newspapers that a local developer had obtained an option to buy the property, with the purpose of converting it into apartments for the elderly. It was quite a jolt, I'll tell you. Our situation was impossible; yet we were still confident that the building would be ours. (Now God could work.)

After further prayer, some of us went to visit the developer. We knew that federal financing for

---

*The story of the acquisition of the Julienne property was told in *Christian Life* magazine, copyright June 1976, Christian Life, Inc., Gundersen Drive & Schmale Road, Wheaton, IL 60187. Reprinted here by permission.

61569.

the conversion would take time to arrange, so we asked, "Do you think that while you're arranging the financing, our school could occupy the building?"

"I don't see why not," he answered. "In fact, I'll approach the Sisters and get them to agree. I will suggest that it be rent-free simply because it should save the Sisters money." (The Sisters were still having to pay for insurance, maintenance, and building security.) He went on, "It might even help me with the local authorities in certain zoning problems if you are occupying the building."

However, he hastened to warn us, "Don't get your hopes up as far as the future is concerned. I have never been turned down when I applied for this type of financing." (The developer, who was also State Chairman of the Democratic Party, had considerable political clout.)

So in July 1973 we moved our junior high and high school classes into the Julienne property, paying utilities, insurance, and other expenses, but no rent! (Praise God!)

A few months later the developer found it impossible to secure the finances necessary to carry out his project. We reentered negotiations with the Sisters of Notre Dame. The fact that the developer had held the option for over six months to buy the property actually gave us another two years to prepare for the purchase. By then we were in a better position to handle the transaction.

In July of 1975 the sale was closed at a purchase price of $750,000, substantially under the developer's original offer. This year we are ministering to some 700 junior high and high school students in the former Julienne building; and the convent has been converted into an elementary school where some 300 youngsters attend daily. In addition, one night a week adult Christian education goes on at this location.

A letter from an alumnus expressed the thoughts of many in reference to our acquisition of these facilities: "I'm glad to hear everything goes well. It certainly is a thrill to see how the Lord works. I remember last year wondering if Mr. Schindler was making some pretty rash statements about DCS getting Julienne High School building. It looked doubtful, but the Lord showed that he was still on the throne."

Of course, a huge building like this, built in the 1920s, presented a real expense when it came to heating. We expected that, but the winter of 1977 was so unusually severe that our situation became critical.

In an effort to conserve natural gas, the governor of Ohio had ordered all schools to close for at least two weeks during the month of January. In our area the Dayton Power and Light Company was particularly short of natural gas, and the situation in the area served by this power company was the most critical in the entire state.

So on February 4 our school, like many other local users, was among those affected by the power company's declaration that all nondomestic users of natural gas cut back to plant protection level until March 21. ("Plant protection level" involves just enough heat to keep water pipes from freezing.)

At an emergency meeting of the school board

on Sunday, February 6, the figure of $42,000 was arrived at as the cost of replacing the natural gas used over the school's allocation with propane, plus the propane necessary to heat the school for the rest of the winter. The facilities we were concerned with were the buildings that made up the former Julienne property, because the building in which our south elementary school was located had already been converted to fuel oil.

When we realized what a steep price we would have to pay to heat with propane, we decided to convert our boilers so they could use either natural gas or fuel oil, which would be cheaper eventually. However, such a conversion might take as long as a month to accomplish; and with the weather so bitterly cold, we could not hold classes during that time.

The next day, Monday, February 7, the other administrators and I began making telephone calls, only to find that securing an oil tank adequate for our needs would take at least three weeks, and suppliers of fuel oil (to fill the tank) doubted that they would even be able to keep their regular customers supplied, much less take on a new one with needs such as ours. Again we were at an impasse with no place to turn except to God.

That night school families met in cottage prayer meetings all over the area. The crowds were not large at these meetings, but the petitions were fervent. We knew we needed God's help in this fuel problem.

And how he began to answer!

The next day we learned that the school board of a south suburb "just happened" to have 16,000 gallons more fuel oil than they needed, and we could buy that . . . *if* we could take delivery that week.

So we began prayerfully searching the Yellow Pages, telephoning dealers to try to find a tank that would be available immediately.

Again, it "just happened" that a local dealer had a 20,000-gallon tank ready for a customer who could no longer take delivery. (This tank was about 100 dollars cheaper than the one that was to be ready in three weeks!)

So far, our efforts had met with remarkable success. *But* the tank had to be in the ground, which was then frozen to a depth of three feet. We told a Christian contractor about this need, and he donated his equipment and men to work two full days and get that huge ten-foot-by-thirty-four-foot tank buried! Another contractor donated sand and gravel and other labor for us.

Next we had to convert the boilers from natural gas to the use of gas or fuel oil. The Lord caused a local salesman to "go to bat" for us. He persistently contacted a firm in Kansas City until it agreed to air freight one burner, enough to handle the heating needs on a temporary basis. (Later another was installed, since our system needs two for ordinary use.)

To this point, the needs seemed to be taken care of in the building where the junior high and high school classes met. But the elementary school which met in what used to be the convent was going to have to operate with a boiler whose burners could not be converted to fuel oil.

Then a Christian engineer suggested that a

steam line be run from the high school building over to the elementary, since the boilers in the high school building were more than adequate to heat both buildings. When we investigated, we discovered that such a line already existed! The previous owners had closed it off with a metal plate, which was easily removed. An electronic valve, which was missing at one end, was found over in a corner on the floor. When we cleaned it up and installed it, it worked beautifully!

As a result, this two-building complex is now heated more efficiently and economically than it was before the energy shortage of that record-breaking winter. And instead of the estimated $42,000 required for one season to heat with propane, the conversion to the cheaper fuel oil cost only $22,000 and should enable us to have lower fuel bills in coming winters.

In the words of the psalmist: "How we laughed and sang for joy. And the other[s] . . . said, 'What amazing things the Lord has done for them.' "[1]

Why do I write about these experiences? To encourage you to look up: when things look black, the Lord has not forgotten you. He means all things for our good when we love him and are following his purpose.[2]

There is yet another story I would like to share. It concerns the ministry of our Thrift Shop. The purchase of the nine acres adjoining our south elementary school included a two-story farmhouse that was built in 1824. We tried renting the house, but somehow that arrangement was never satisfactory. So in 1972 some volunteers from our school family set up a Thrift Shop in the old house. Our goal was to make good quality clothing, shoes, and household items available at very low prices.

The idea began to catch on among our school families. Many fine quality items were brought to us by those who no longer needed them. As a result, word began to spread that people could find good bargains at our shop.

Many families from the metropolitan area came and outfitted their children for school, purchased toys and Christmas decorations, or picked up some household goods they needed— all at a fraction of what new items would cost.

The staff has always been careful to present a positive Christian testimony. Often it is possible to share a word of faith with a customer, and sometimes tracts are put into customers' sacks.

When the Thrift Shop workers learn of extreme needs, merchandise is given free. Several families who have been victims of fires have received help from our shop; and we also had opportunity to minister to many who suffered from the tornado which devastated Xenia, Ohio, in 1974.

The City Mission of downtown Dayton has often received clothing from our shop, especially since they have begun to minister to women as well as men. And occasionally when the shop is overstocked on certain items or when the merchandise needs repair before it can be used, these items are donated to the Salvation Army or to Goodwill.

Our school has never had a really large donor. God has not seen fit to send one our way; but last year the Thrift Shop turned over a total of

$33,000 as a result of the merchandise it had sold. How we appreciate the faithful work of our volunteers who keep the shop open, ministering to people in a very practical way. It is remarkable to me that this ministry has become a truly "large donor" in helping meet the financial needs of our school!

Maybe miracle is a strong word to use when I speak of these experiences, but certainly they are *wonderful!*

NOTES

CHAPTER ONE

1. 1 Corinthians 6:17.
2. Watchman Nee, *The Latent Power of the Soul* (New York: Christian Fellowship Publishers Inc., 1972), p. 7.
3. John 16:13.
4. William J. Lanouette, "The 4th R is Religion," *The National Observer* (January 15, 1977).
5. 1 Kings 3:5-14.
6. Proverbs 3:13-26.
7. Proverbs 4:7.
8. Philippians 2:5.

CHAPTER TWO

1. John F. Blanchard, Jr., "Can We Live with Public Education?" *Moody Monthly* (October 1971), p. 88.
2. *Ibid.*
3. *Ibid.*
4. James 1:17; Hebrews 13:8.
5. Jeremiah 17:9.
6. Blanchard, p. 89.
7. "Special Report—Terror in Schools," *U.S. News & World Report* (January 26, 1976), p. 52.
8. George H. Gallup, "Eighth Annual Gallup Poll of the Public's Attitudes Toward the Public Schools," reprinted from the October 1976 *Phi Delta Kappan*.
9. *Ibid.*

NOTES

10. John D. Jess, The Chapel of the Air broadcast (December 2, 1970), Wheaton, IL 60187.
11. *Op. cit.*, Wm. J. Lanouette.
12. Acts 2:41–47.
13. Ephesians 4:14.
14. *Are They . . . Sheltered?*, Dayton Christian Schools, Inc., Dayton, OH 45405.
15. *Ibid.*
16. *Ibid.*

CHAPTER THREE
1. Dr. Roy Zuck as quoted by Paul A. Kienel in *The Christian School: Why It Is Right for Your Child* (Wheaton, IL: Victor Books, 1974), p. 73.
2. Colossians 2:8.
3. Jay E. Adams, *The Big Umbrella*, (Grand Rapids, Mich.: Baker Book House, 1972), p. 249.
4. Dr. Frank E. Gaebelein, *The Pattern of God's Truth* (Chicago: Moody Press, 1968), p. 37.
5. Luke 6:40, NASB.
6. Adams, p. 258.

CHAPTER FOUR
1. Addresses of these associations are as follows:
   American Association of Christian Schools
   6601 N.W. 167th Street
   Hialeah (Miami), FL 33015

   Association of Christian Schools International
   P.O. Box 4097
   Whittier, CA 90607

   Eastern Association of Christian Schools
   6707 Woodyard Road
   Upper Marlboro, MD 20870

   National Association of Christian Schools
   Box 28
   Wheaton, IL 60187

   National Union of Christian Schools
   865 Twenty-Eighth, Southeast
   Grand Rapids, MI 49508
2. Dr. A.J. Gordon as quoted by Mary Goforth Moynan in "The Power of Prayer," *Everybody*, World Literature Crusade (Vol. 3, No. 8, August 1977), p. 22.

CHAPTER FIVE
1. WACS students are compared to some 225,000 students that were carefully selected to represent average students across the United States (1973). The figures represent the average (median) of all tests at each grade level. The test used was the 1973

109

Stanford Achievement Test, Form A. Western Association of Christian Schools, P.O. Box 4097, Whittier, CA 90607.

2. Scores based on the 1973 Stanford Test of Academic Skills, Level I, Form A. Western Association of Christian Schools, P.O. Box 4097, Whittier, CA 90607.

3. Jeremiah 9:23, 24, *The Amplified Bible* (Grand Rapids, Mich.: Zondervan Publishing House, 1965).

4. 1 Thessalonians 5:23.

5. *Character Sketches*, Institute in Basic Youth Conflicts, Inc., First Edition, Rand McNally, 1976, p. 11.

6. Isaiah 55:8, 9.

7. Genesis 3:5, 6.

8. Romans 16:19, *Amplified Bible*.

9. Matthew 6:33.

10. Philippians 4:8.

11. Proverbs 23:7.

12. Richard C. Halverson, *Perspective*, Concern, Inc., 5500 River Road, Washington, DC 20016 (Vol. XXVII, No. 4), February 19, 1975.

13. Proverbs 4:23, *Amplified Bible*.

14. Harry Blemires, *The Christian Mind* (London: S.P.C.K., 1966), pp. 3, 4, as quoted by Dr. Paul A. Kienel, *Christian School Comment*, WACS, P.O. Box 4097, Whittier, CA 90607.

15. Halverson (Vol. XXVII, No. 22), October 29, 1975.

16. The Institute for Athletic Perfection, P.O. Box 2021, Prescott, AZ 86301.

17. Institute in Basic Youth Conflicts, Inc., Box 1, Oak Brook, IL 60521, has a list of positive character qualities with their definitions.

18. John C. Whitcomb, Foreword to *Education for the Real World*, Henry M. Morris (San Diego, CA: Creation Life Publishers), 1977).

19. Adams, p. 255.

CHAPTER SIX

1. Brother Lawrence, *The Practice of the Presence of God*, a Spire Book published by Pyramid Publications for Fleming H. Revell, Old Tappan, NJ, 1958, pp. 22, 23.

2. *Ibid.*, p. 24.

3. *Ibid.*, p. 8.

4. Job 23:10.

5. 1 Thessalonians 5:18.

6. John 17:21.

7. John 13:35.

8. Karen Ann Wojahn, "A Conversation with Sherwood Wirt," *Christian Herald* (October 1977), p. 92.

9. Proverbs 16:28.

10. Richard Ellsworth, *The Shadow of the Broad Brim* (Valley Forge, PA: The Judson Press, 1934), p. 26.

NOTES

CHAPTER SEVEN
1. Romans 13:1-7; 1 Timothy 2:1-3.
2. Galatians 5:22, 23.
3. JoAn Summers, *Fruitbasket Friends* (Plainfield, NJ: Logos International, 1975).

John M. Drescher, *Spirit Fruit* (Scottdale, PA: Herald Press, 1974).

I Learn About the Fruit of the Holy Spirit, Marie and Peter Chapian (Carol Stream, IL: Creation House, 1974).

The Music Machine, a Musical Adventure Teaching the Fruit of the Spirit to All Ages, Birdwing Records, a Division of Sparrow Records, Inc., 8587 Canoga Ave., Canoga Park, CA 91304.
4. Evangelism to Communist Lands, Box 303, Glendale, CA 91209.

CHAPTER EIGHT
1. Psalm 126:2, *The Living Bible.*
2. Romans 8:28.